A PAIR OF SEDONA MIRACLES

Life as Seen by Sam and Athena
a Pair of Hybrids in a Land of Conformity

MICHAEL AND LINDA HARRIS

Copyright © 2019 by Michael and Linda Harris.771236
Library of Congress Control Number: 2019900177

ISBN: Softcover   978-1-9845-7574-6
        Hardcover   978-1-9845-7575-3
        EBook   978-1-9845-7573-9

Print information available on the last page

Rev. date: 01/11/2019

To order additional copies of this book, contact:
Xlibris
1-888-795-4274
www.Xlibris.com
Orders@Xlibris.com

A Pair of Sedona Miracles

Life as seen by Sam and Athena
A Pair of Hybrids in a Land of Conformity
Michael and Linda Kay Harris

Sam and Athena at Play

Contents

I would like to thank the following individuals who either helped with this manuscript or were influential in some manner to its origination.

Lisa Hanard, whose unique pictures adorn both the cover and interior, and who provided tremendous insight and emotional support that all three of us needed to make this happen.

Angela Abel, whose long time friendship has enhanced the lives of all three of us, and who continues to provide support and friendship, and

let's not forget Milo, Sam's longtime hiking buddy and Athena's boyfriend.

Sam and Athena's hiking partners, including Milo, Stella, Zelda, Jax, Pup and most recently Marli, for helping teach Sam and Athena how to behave a bit more like a dog and less like a wild animal.

And most importantly, Linda Kay, my wife and Sam and Athena's favorite female human, who added her hard work and personality to this manuscript.

Sam can be reached at this e-mail address shown on his web page:

themiracleofsam.com, info@themiracleofsam.com

and also Facebook: Sam Harris

This book is dedicated to
Sam
who saved my life,
and to
Linda Kay
who makes life worth living,
and to
Athena, who continues the legacy.

Sam and Athena Swimming

A Pair of Sedona Miracles

Sam was the first to arrive. He came into the word in the usual way, but something was different. His mom was a Golden Retriever living in a puppy mill in a place called West Sedona, and his dad was a migrating coyote who found mom too much to resist.

Sam's siblings were all perfect little Golden babies, but Sam looked a bit different. He had dad's eyes, face, lithe body and the inherited knowledge that comes from a lifetime of living off the land, all gifts from his dad, who was a leader in the coyote community. Sam was the first to walk, first to talk, and the first to learn what happens when you do something bad. His appearance and behavior got him a one-way ticket to the local animal shelter.

Nine years later, nearly to the day, Athena was hiking somewhere in the Village of Oak Creek, a Sedona suburb, when she was captured and taken to the very same shelter. She was the child of a domesticated Siberian Husky, and a wild Mexican Grey wolf. The union was intentionally created by a breeder who lived outside of the Arizona area, at the request of an Arizona family.

The busy family quickly realized Athena was a bit too much to handle for a working couple with kids, all of whom spent the majority of their day off-site. Athena found lots to do, none of it consistent with the family's greater good. When she finally escaped one day--one of many that is, they called a friend in to find her and deposit her in the shelter.

How Sam came to us:

Sam spent the next eighteen months in and out of various homes; each one of them tied him to a tree in the front or back yard and left him there all day, alone and without any level of attention, love or affection. Being the resourceful pup he was, he quickly escaped each one of these forms of confinement, winding up back at the pound for the fourth time in January of the year 2009. The last time he came back to the kennels, he still had a piece of the rope, which he had chewed through, around his neck.

That's where Linda and I came into the picture…

Linda and I had a terrible 2008, with huge financial damage, which culminated with the loss of our precious Golden Retriever Sarah to Valley Fever near the end of December. Linda felt it might be a good idea to peruse the local humane society to find a new friend, though I was pretty much out of it and not too enthusiastic.

I was at a personal low when I first met Sam. He looked sadly over the small gate at the humane society kennel, and stood on his back feet, leaning against the gate as we reviewed the various options available. He never barked or whined, and was conspicuously silent above the loud barking and high noise level. He was in for his 4th visit to the kennel since his birth, and obviously didn't care for the noise and high level of activity going on around him. I think we both were ready for a change to the good. It goes without saying that we kind of took to each other, and he came home with us.

Now for Athena:

One of our good friends, who I shall call Bonnie, was aware of the situation surrounding Athena's plight, and let Linda and I know about the situation. We visited the shelter with Sam in tow, and spent a bit of time with Athena, who was a year and a day old at that time. Sam, Linda, Athena and I agreed that she should come home with us.

Both times we brought a hybrid pup into our established home, we carefully studied their habits and behavior, making allowances to support both halves of their psyches. The dog halves were easy, but both Sam and Athena had special needs, and as we spent more time together, we understood what they needed beyond the traditional pet-master relationship. Both required and still need some time to be in nature, hiking three to five miles every day in an open area where they could nurture and practice their wild sides. Sam and Athena had to determine their respective places in the family model as well. Athena, the Warrior Princess, constantly tests the fences with Sam, who often gives her just enough latitude to satisfy her needs. As you will observe in this book about their daily activities, neither one of them has a distinctive upper hand. This works for all of us, and a harmonic relationship has developed that works for Linda, me, Sam and Athena.

Please enjoy this look into the lives of Sam and Athena, and those of us who play and live with this unique pair of miracles.

Sam and Athena on the Hunt

Sam's Trip Home

CHAPTER 1
Sam

Some stories are about humans and their struggles with adaptability. Some are not.

These tales about Coydog Sam and Wolf Hybrid Athena fall into the second category.

Both Sam and Athena were born into a strange world of order and conformity, a place neither of their wild sides would normally ever have to endure. These stories describe pictorially and in writing how a pair of hybrids learn lessons in love and adaptability from a constantly-increasing pack of humans and their canine companions, all while traveling about in the beautiful venue called Sedona.

Why did we write this book?

Humans hold a special place in this world. We share unique abilities to make life better for everything that holds space on this planet, by protecting and preserving resources which support and maintain all life here. Humans, in turn, are given the gift of friendship and companionship by the other creatures, particularly canine based ones, who historically have been our benefactors, friends and life companions through the ages.

This book is about several humans and canine-based creatures that share love and company with each other while enjoying and sharing resources available in the area called Sedona. Please enjoy and share the stories herein with friends, family and anyone else who will bend an ear in your general direction.

This book of short stories starts with Sam. He began his life with us after we made a brief stop at the local animal shelter where he was dropped off by his mother's owners. More details on Sam's early life can be found in the book titled "The Miracle of Sam".

Sam's mother was a Golden Retriever. She was paid a visit by a wily Coyote who was captivated by Sam's mom, and spent the night. Shortly thereafter, she provided her owners with a batch of little baby puppies.

All but one of the puppies were perfect images of mom, all but Sam. He was different in appearance and behavior, being the first of the puppies to walk, the first to obtain nourishment, and the first to find a way out of the enclosure housing the babies. Unfortunately, due to his nonconformist appearance and behavior, he was also the first to be sent away from home. He would wind up in the local animal shelter because of these differences.

Sam's First Hike

After a short acquaintance meeting at the shelter with Mike and Linda, Sam knew he had found the ideal packmates. A short walk outside to the waiting vehicle followed.

Sam willingly jumped into the Jeep. He knew things were looking up. For some reason, he bonded quickly with Mike and Linda, anticipating good times and new experiences. The emotional first acquaintance meeting at the shelter is all it took.

The name the shelter gave him, taken from Sam's hangout when he escaped the first three adoptees, was Buddha. That name went away, and he was renamed by Mike after Big Sam McCord, founder of the Bonanza mine in Alaska. (The song "North to Alaska" played on in the background, signaling approval of Sam's new moniker.)

Sam's first day started with a short hike, which bonded the pack even more. Sam was at home in the forest and enjoyed the romp with his new packmates Mike and Linda. It was the first of many more such adventures. Sam was able to hike almost every day afterward, and finally had the freedom his coyote half needed to survive.

Evening at the family domicile brought a calm Sam had never experienced. Gone was the constant din associated with the shelter, and the complete solitude associated with his experiences living in the great outdoors vanished as well.

After the first hike, and pretty much ever after, Sam found a peace and calm that allowed him to have a completely restful sleep during the night. This was a completely new experience for him. While he was living outside alone, his den was visited nocturnally by anything big enough to eat him, including an annoying pack of coyotes that called Buddha Beach home. The rock overhang protecting his den had numerous scratches embedded upon it from the hungry claws attached to several big coyotes.

Sam Passed Out

After living with Mike and Linda for a year, Sam got to revisit his old home at Buddha Beach. He showed Mike his den, and then brought forth from within the playthings he had amassed over the 18-month stay there. A well-chewed water bottle, one toy, some short pieces of wood he used to teethe upon and a few unrecognizable artifacts came from within.

Sam brought the toy home and after a trip through the washer and dryer it appeared good as new. To this day he still brings it out occasionally, presumably to remind him of where he once lived and how long ago that was.

As it turns out, Sam began to embrace the Sedona spiritual lifestyle, and had a particularly efficient method of finding related artifacts in the strangest of places. He located some hippie artifactual materials somewhere between Bell Rock Pathway and Llama Trail one day and immediately showed Mike, who photographed them and left them as they were found. Why mess with karma, both Sam and Mike decided.

Sam's Spiritually Infused Findings

In addition to this gift of finding small artifacts, Sam acquired the capability to locate unique items, things that were left here long ago by visitors or prior denizens of the red rock wilderness surrounding the village of Sedona. Many travelers moved through this area, both recently and long ago. As they migrated from the area, items which no longer held value were left behind, presumably to amuse and astound those fortunate enough to find them many years afterward.

One such maverick was Harry Templeton. He lived off the land for many years in the area between what is now called the Village, and the small community called Hillside.

A hiker who leaves the current trails and bushwhacks a bit will most likely come upon some of the things Harry and others like him left behind. In fact, some of Templeton Trail still has parts of some of his vehicles embedded in the trail, as well as remains of at least one of his home-like enclosures alongside the trail.

This huge thing was deposited in a wilderness area at least five miles from the nearest road, which at the time was a small dirt road located approximately beneath the right-hand component of the bifurcated Hwy 179 scenic road connecting the Village of Oak Creek and Sedona.

More of Sam's Findings

Some of Sam's findings touch on the ancient visitors and residents of the Sedona area who came, lived here for a time, and suddenly disappeared. All that remains to remind us of them are ancient dwellings in the rocks, and some of the artwork they considered too cumbersome to take with them. These artifacts can be found while hiking in the area. If you have trouble locating these, local land managers or USFS personnel are happy to give you directions, as well as advise on how best to enjoy the Sedona area.

Sam Finds a Cave Dwelling

Having a unique creature like Sam living with us requires a change in how you plan your time. You should expect to spend several hours a day somewhere in the forest, as Sam will do so with or without you in tow. Sam's first few days with us showed him we had the desire to make him a wonderful home, and more important, spend lots of time outdoors. I am certain that is why he didn't take off for parts unknown the first few days he lived with us.

Sam's nickname at the shelter was "Escape Artist" and his activity level was labeled "Rock and Roll", so we knew what we were in for when he came home with us. Fortunately for us, his requirements fit our capabilities and the union was a wonderful thing for all involved. Linda and I often say we didn't save Sam, he saved us. He arrived at a time when we were in a very bad way, and suddenly everything changed for the better.

When we first found Sam at the shelter, we were advised he had escaped three prior adoptees at least one time each. He liked living on the land, as his father's pack did, and though he had to make this journey alone, he was ok with his decision. Living alone taught him one thing though—he preferred company, but it had to be the right company. We are extremely fortunate Sam chose us as his packmates.

Sam came to us with a wealth of local knowledge. He was eager to show us things he had located which interested and captivated him. Sometimes we would all jump into the Jeep and drive until Sam gave an indication we should stop and smell the roses. Once we stopped, he would take us into the wilderness and suddenly we would see something amazing. Here are a couple of examples.

Sam Introduces Us to Ancient Artwork

A bit further down the path, even more magnificent artwork could be found. Sam was amusing himself with some small aquatic creature that looked like a crayfish as we walked down the huge wash with the most magnificent ancient pictorial elements we have ever seen.

Bear Paws

Coyote

One sunny and warm morning, Sam decided to share a very special place with us. He had found this beautiful location on an excursion for food. During that trip, he found a group of working dogs. After the customary introductions were over, he snuck in with some of the more playful cattle dogs and followed them, participating in their daily activities. The dogs had a huge working area, which covered some interesting and beautiful parts of the Sedona landscape.

During that workday, which provided Sam a nice meal and plenty of clean water, Sam wandered off and found a nice shady area with a strange and powerful energy. While resting there, he felt the presence of a family of native Americans who were long gone. Their strength of character allowed a bit of them to remain behind, and Sam picked up on this wonderful positive energy.

He never forgot this place, and often returned when he felt a bit down, and wanted company. The presence there gave him strength and developed his intuitive capability to the point where he no longer had to wonder what humans wanted of him. That capability is probably one of the gifts that allows him to survive and grow in the human dominated world in which he currently resides.

Sam's Special Place

Sam had yet another surprise for us. In a small area where cattle dominate the landscape and the occasional coyote pack yearns for a meal consisting of slow newborns, our little Coydog learned self-defense tactics and found another power spot where he could recharge his batteries. Of course, he was eager to show off his find.

We turned him lose once inside the fenced enclosure, and he trotted up the rugged Jeep road toward a small trailhead few people have ever seen. No evidence of vehicle traffic was evident, and for good reason. We dropped the Jeep through a huge set of formidable sharp washed out areas and proceeded forward.

A Trip to The Monolith

We hiked around three miles on what looked like a cattle trail, with an occasional horse footprint evident, but no foot traffic. As we approached a high spot, the entire perspective of the terrain changed. Volcanic rock and debris were replaced by extremely green grass and other dense foliage. In the middle of a small rise in the terrain a unique volcanic formation could be found. It was alone on the hillside, and from this vantage point a human could look upon Cathedral Rock, Bell Rock and everything in between. It was an amazing site.

That alone would have been worth the hike, but there was much more. The lone rock, upon further inspection, told a story of wandering people and this landmark was clearly a beacon for them. Upon one side of the monolith was a timeline or calendar, and on the north face some very worn petroglyphs of deer, javelina, various reptiles and other mammals. This was a wonderful find, but in addition, when you sat in a certain spot on the formation, you could feel power and lightness of being emanate from it. This is now a spot we frequently seek when we are feeling a bit off or just need recharging. Thank you for sharing this with us Sam!

Sam's Power Spot

Not far from the monolith we found another artifact. Sam walked us behind a huge dome where the denizens of the past used to perform a pot breaking ceremony. The land around this dome is scattered with pottery shards of all types and sizes, including red/black, black/white, black only, red only and white only. It is an amazing site to visit, and one we will keep to ourselves until the land manager decides what to do with it.

Within twenty feet of this site are several pottery kilns dug into the side of a seasonal wash. More pottery shards can be found there. On a rise just above the kilns we found what appears to be the remnants of a Tipi. It is the only structure which resembles a dwelling within ten miles of this area.

Tipi

Sam in the Pottery Kiln

We were very grateful to Sam for this gift. He in turn was happy to share with his new pack something they could enjoy and treasure. The give-take relationship we developed with Sam taught both species something about the other, and cemented a relationship built on mutual trust, love and admiration. Many years later, when Athena came into the picture, the tools we developed during our time with Sam became invaluable in helping us understand and accept Athena's wild side, and love her.

Pottery Shards

Sam's Sense of Snow

We had been with Sam less than a month when it snowed enough to stick, and then some. We were a bit concerned how he would react, but quickly realized he was not only familiar with, but enthusiastic about the event. A hop in the Jeep and short drive later and we were the only ones on the forest. No one was on the road as far as we could see, as the conditions were extreme for the Sedona area. In other words, it was a perfect day in the forest.

Sam Enjoying the Snow

Ditto

One More

Sam's sense of snow turned out one day to be an invaluable gift. On a freezing and cloudy day in early 2010, after a significant snowfall that blanketed the Sedona area, we were out and about near the area called Turkey Creek. When we pulled into the lower parking lot, we noticed a snow-covered car that had obviously been there overnight. The car was not occupied, but a pair of tracks could be seen on the trail that leads out the southwest corner towards the saddle.

Again, ours were the only vehicle tracks, and no one was driving anywhere. It seems Sedona becomes impassable to most when a few inches of snow drop, unless one has a Jeep in their vehicle inventory. We drove to the upper trailhead and parked near the State Park entrance.

It wasn't long before we found them. A couple from somewhere in California had taken the notion they could play in the snow for a few hours just before sunset and successfully get back to their waiting automobile. By the tracks we found, they had wandered around for about three miles in erratic circular motion, with no idea where to go. The evening had not helped, as it had lightly snowed all night, and the couple had no idea how to read the moonlight. It had been good country dark all evening, which did not help them either. Neither did their AT&T phones with no signal.

Sam found them first while chasing something that looked like a rabbit, only faster. He quickly got my attention, and we were able to walk them to the Jeep and drive them to their awaiting vehicle. I gave them a quick check over and a couple of bottles of water and sent them to ready-care, where I am assuming someone read them the riot act and gave them some common sense advise regarding hiking in the snow.

Sam and Coyotes

Our little boy is the byproduct of an interlude between two different species. Mom was a beautiful Golden Retriever and Dad was a handsome Coyote male who came looking for something to eat and left as a father. Sam was born in the usual way, and had several brothers and sisters, all of whom looked like Mom. Sam, however, shared both Mom and Dad's features and intellect, and as a result, was rejected by the puppy mill and accepted by the local shelter.

While in escape mode, Sam lived on the land, and had a nice den in the Buddha Beach area near West Sedona. While there, he experienced the social bias associated with being part dog, and he was classified as a food group by his dad's kind. This gave Sam a huge bias against coyotes which remains part of him today.

There have been many instances while hiking with us where Sam has displayed his dislike of coyotes. The first was just after we adopted him. A group of coyotes approached us from below while we were on a cliffside. Sam saw them well before they knew of his presence and waited until they were in range. Then he leaped off the cliff and surprised them by dropping into the middle of the group.

Sam Surprising a Coyote Pack

Once within the coyote pack, Sam inspected each face. When he was satisfied he had the leader in his sights, he grabbed him by the neck and tossed the boss to the ground. The pack leader did not move, though he was unharmed. As Sam walked around the still boss, the other coyotes backed off and disappeared. Only after they were long gone did Sam allow the pack leader to exit quietly and with his remaining dignity. This behavior has repeated itself several times since the first occurrence. Sam was finally free of the fear his initial coyote experiences forced upon him.

Sam is particularly vigilant when other pups are in the picture. He will monitor movements and behaviors of all creatures in the area, and then react accordingly if anything captures his attention. If he hears anything indicating a predator is in the proximity, he is usually the first to act on correcting the situation.

Sam Prepares for the Chase

Note in the picture above that the two dogs are preparing to chase a rabbit that is just behind the small bush to their right, while the full measure of Sam's sense is focused on the coyote atop the hill above the trio. Moments later, Sam launched at the coyote, who along with its hidden subordinates, took flight. It was only about a second before Sam caught them, accompanied by his two reluctant canine companions. The coyotes continued their exit strategy at high speed, and Sam let them escape unharmed.

About three minutes after the brief chase, the coyotes sounded off from a nearby hill, triumphantly telling tall tales to anyone willing to listen of their triumphant escape from the devil dogs in the valley. Sam listened, smiling, and relayed to his two hiking companions his hard-learned techniques of evasion and the numerous attack strategies he used to eliminate coyote meetup issues. They listened intently, knowing other such events would occur, and felt a bit safer and more confident after the discourse.

They heard the coyotes again on the return trip from the long hike. Each member of the hiking pack sighed, knowing that this group of predators would give the three musketeers,

Sam, Stella and Zelda, a wide berth both now and in the conceivable future as they travelled within this sparsely forested part of the Sedona landscape.

Sam Finds Other Things

One thing Sam is particularly good at finding is biological entities who have found themselves disoriented and are having some difficulty determining how to get back to their version of reality. Sam and I, when it was just the two of us, often hiked the less traversed trails in search of excitement in whatever form it took on that given day. Often the excitement centered around giving lost travelers of the forest a point in the right direction, or occasionally medical assistance. This was going to be one of those mornings.

Sam With Lost Boy

As we started our excursion at a popular trailhead in the West Sedona area, a couple approached us frantically speaking in broken English. They were clearly not from around here, both dressed in sweaters with the temperature in the eighty-something range.

I gathered from the couple that their son had wandered off and neither of them had access to a communication device which worked in this demographic region. Fearing one of them would get lost as well, the couple awaited help from anyone who would happen by, which meant Sam and me.

The man had hiked all over the immediate area and had come back with the boy's mittens and nothing else. It was early Tuesday morning and everyone else except us was presumably sitting down to a hearty country breakfast.

I watched Sam. He was looking toward the creek, which I took as not a good omen. The water was moving much too fast for anyone to attempt a crossing. Hopefully the boy didn't make that mistake.

I asked the man to turn one of the mittens inside out and let Sam take a sniff, which Sam readily did. Then Sam went for a hike of his own, paralleling the racing creek on our side of the flow.

As we followed, we could see an occasional footprint of the correct size, indicating the boy had gone in the general direction the stream was flowing, with Sam's huge footprints following the trail. I noticed rocks dislodged from their resting place several times, suggesting the boy had practiced the fine art of rock skipping.

In the distance, I could hear an excited voice, and Sam playing in the water. A sigh of relief came from me, and the chattering couple walking alongside me became even more excited, taking off at an extremely fast trot in the direction of the noises.

I will never forget the picture of Sam walking the boy back to the trailhead. When I relayed the story to an artist friend, she painted a depiction of the scene in such a manner as to protect the identity of the young fellow. The morning sun painted a tapestry of unique beauty as the boy and dog walked together along the damp creek, and the artist caught the image perfectly.

I heard back from the couple once they returned home had a chance to recover. The boy wanted to know more about his rescuer Sam, so I sent them a copy of Sam's book, "The Miracle of Sam" with the details of their story included. I was careful not to include any specifics that would identify the exact location or any information that could identify the participants when recounting the exciting adventure.

I have given my artist friend credit in this book's forward, as she richly deserves. I'm pleased to recognize her and several photographer's contributions as well, as this book would not have been possible without their extremely creative efforts. In addition, Linda

Kay, my spouse has written several of the stories in her own valuable words. Please enjoy her stories as well as mine, as both come from the heart and our love for the subjects of this book.

Introducing Sam's Hiking Friends, and Athena

Now that you have a brief introduction to Sam, you will discover the diversified types of friendships he shares with his fellow hiking buddies, and his sister Athena. For more details on Sam's early life, please read **The Miracle of Sam**, available in print or e-book from Amazon.com. Sam can currently be reached at either one of his two e-mail addresses: info@themiracleofsam.com or m.marinetic@gmail.com. In addition, his webpage is *themiracleofsam.com.*

Sam has some regular buddies with whom he spends quality forest time. A brief introduction to a few of them follows, and after this chapter, more detailed information and some of the many adventures shared by these pack members can be found.

Sam and Linda

Linda was the first person to allow Sam to hike without limits. She opened the door to his wild side on their first hike together, and by doing so, Linda set the standards others who took Sam out to play would have to meet.

Sam learned quickly he was allowed and encouraged to let his wild side come out, and this freedom is one of the things which bonded him to our family. Since Linda and I encouraged the mutual friendship we shared with Sam, he gave back love and strength at a time when we needed it most, and this gift from Sam saved us in a time of terrible crisis. Sam's life strength and the examples he set in early life showed us many of the tasks we considered unsurmountable were achievable if we worked hard enough and were consistent in our efforts.

Linda and Sam Hiking

Angie and Milo

Milo was one of the first dogs Sam befriended while experiencing the first aspects of his introduction to human-based activities. A trip to the local dog park seemed the best way to see if Sam could acclimate to the presence of dogs and their owners. Fortunately, his brief introduction to canines at the Sedona Animal Shelter helped him make the transition from predator to playful companion.

Sam quickly became the father figure for many of the less aggressive pups at the park. He sat on a grassy knoll near one side of the enclosure and monitored activities. If things got out of line, he would quickly get in the midst of the activity, breaking up any canine disagreements he deemed inappropriate.

Every evening before the sun set we would head over to the dog park. Once Sam entered, all the smaller dogs would follow him to the grassy knoll, where Sam and his followers would sit and watch activities. Any dog that wanted to engage in play would make its selection from this safe vantage point, and once done, would return to safety.

One day, Angie decided to bring Milo to the dog park. Milo is huge but very timid when it comes to aggressive behavior, and several of the more spirited dogs decided to give him a welcome not unlike the first day of a newbie in any Federal Penitentiary. Sam watched for a bit, and then descended on the aggressors, scattering them to the four winds. From that day on, Sam and Milo were best buds.

Angie, Linda and I became friends as well. Whenever she is in town, Milo and Angie become part of the Sam Hiking experience, and everyone enjoys a day in the forest.

Sam, Milo and Angie

Angie Knows Stuff

I quickly found out that Angie, a USFS employee with immeasurable local trail experience, knew bunches of fun places to hike. She took us to many fun places where few other people could be found, and that suited Sam and Milo just fine. The Boys could cavort and race around and enjoy the scenery, and then find some water in which to play and cool off. I learned a great deal of valuable trail knowledge as well.

Sam and Milo

Once we visited Angie and Milo while they were stationed in Kanab. The trip resulted in a most exceptional visit to The Wave, a feature with very limited access. The lottery turned out in our favor that week, and this picture shows in detail how well a USFS employee can stick to the most extreme features with the greatest of ease. Every time I look at the picture I am reminded of how amazing this brief hike was, and how many other beautiful places there are in the American wilderness.

Angie

The Others

In addition to Sam's special friend Milo, he enjoys hiking with several other creatures of the human and canine persuasions. Here are some of those who were brave enough to spend some quality time with a Coyote hybrid.

Bonnie and the Pups

Local photographer Bonnie has been a good friend for more than a decade, and during that time, we have gone on numerous bike rides and hikes with the pups. She has one wolf hybrid named Stella, an Alaskan Husky named Zelda, and a Golden who is just called Pup. Add Sam to the mix and the afternoon of hiking becomes a unique adventure.

Marty and the Pups

Marty and the Pups

Once upon a time the VVCC President Marty used to hike with Sam and the group. The self-proclaimed water boy, Marty always had enough water to go around, as seen in the previous picture. He finally had to quit hiking with us due to back problems from carrying several hundred ounces of water, the minimum the dogs and hybrids required. He resumed biking instead, which presumably is much better on the spine.

In addition, Marty's propensity to get into precarious positions may have been incentive to reduce his hiking. Many feel biking is less dangerous, but I disagree. Adding the variable of balancing something moving fast gives one an additional fear factor for me to overcome. Many hikers agree it is much easier to go up something than go back down. I feel the following picture is indicative of this belief.

Marty in a Most Peculiar Situation

Athena, the Goddess of War

One day while Bon and I were hiking the pups in October 2016, she got a call that changed our lives forever. (Linda, Sam and me, that is).

A friend of hers told the sad story of a local couple who had decided they wanted a wolf hybrid, and then went as far as to have one intentionally bred. This is never a good idea, especially if the couple has children and work every day as well. They brought the young female home, and then went to work. When they got home, the house was unrecognizable, and the wolf-dog had escaped and was wandering the neighborhood. This happened several times, and as a result, the hybrid wound up at our local pet shelter. I spoke to Linda about the option of adopting her, and we had a few discussions before considering a sister for Sam. Several days had passed before Linda and I went to the shelter and rescued Athena, and she was indeed a piece of work by the time we got to her.

Linda was in the hospital getting chemotherapy for a bone disease while I worked with Athena to teach her basic people skills, and it was a while before she would allow us to touch her enough to assess her physical condition. The original owners had apparently beaten her to keep her quiet, and she sustained a knee injury as a result, and one of her legs was under-developed due to malnutrition. Fortunately, Athena partially adapted to the injuries, and both medicine and proper nourishment took care of the rest.

Athena With Sam

I wouldn't be accurate if I said Sam embraced Athena immediately. It took a bit of time for him to accept and love his new sister. She was initially a resource hog, and Sam didn't initially appreciate sharing his family of eleven years with a stranger.

He did finally welcome her into the pack, and now they hunt and hike as one unit, each anticipating the actions and movements of the other. It is amazing to see, especially when they are helping Coyotes understand their revised boundaries in the forest area Sam and Athena call home.

Escape Artist

When we first picked up Sam, an index card on his cage identified his activity level as *rock and roll*, and his demeanor as *escape artist*. Athena completely redefined these descriptions.

Our little girl has the knack of disappearing while in plain sight, a behavior that often sends us looking everywhere for her, much to Sam's dismay. He sighs and watches as we run around calling her name, and just as we give up, she reappears as if nothing had happened. She has boundless energy and spares no effort in evading containment.

She practices this behavior occasionally while in the forest. One time recently she sent a friend who was babysitting her while I was recovering from a knee replacement into a state of distress for several hours. He looked for her until he got tired, and then gave us a call. With less than eight hours on my new knee, I had to join the search, and found her several miles from where she was last seen. The next day, I ordered a tracking device with a ten-mile radius for her to wear.

Athena's Tracking Collar

I would like to say the proper amount of discipline and training cured Athena of this behavior, but the wolf in her rejects this approach, so on this point we give her a lot of leeway. Sam was very much the same way when he first came to live with us, often scaling the wall during the evening to play in the golf course and chase off coyotes. He eventually discarded this behavior in order to save enough energy so that he could have a great morning hike. We are in hopes Athena will do the same over time.

That said, our little girl has come a long way in the year or two we have enjoyed her company. Her nocturnal behavior is more Sam-like now and she has finally started eating with the rest of the pack, rather than saving room for whatever she could catch while hiking or stalking around in the heavy backyard foliage. She is definitely an Alpha female, and those accompanying characteristics will most positively remain a part of her behavior pattern.

Marli and Her Pack

Lisa, my daughter, and her husband Marcel joined the pack well before Marli was part of their family. I am convinced they fell in love with the idea of a canine companion while hiking with Bon, Sam and the pups one day. It was shortly before Athena became part of the hiking pack that Lisa began to consider the option of another Hanard family member.

Lisa Hiking with Bon and the Pups

Not long after Athena arrived in the summer of 2016, Marcel and Lisa found their canine soul mate Marli. While Athena was acclimating into our household, Marli was experiencing the same thing at the Hanard family residence.

Athena's First Day with Sam

Marcel began to train Marli to behave, and they expanded her training to include skills normally exercised by professional pups in a competitive environment. Little did Marli realize her training would be significantly changed in the presence of Sam and Athena. It didn't take Marli long to find her spot in the pack, and Athena helped her get there as Sam watched, pleased at the remarkable progress.

Athena Trains Marli

It wasn't long before Marli became acclimated, just as Athena had done a short time before. Marli is quite the athlete, and now gives both Athena and Sam quite a run for the money.

Marli Pursuing Athena

Athena Talking to Coyotes

A few days ago, after hiking up several hundred feet of steep rocky terrain to reach an ancient Native American ceremonial plateau near the Village, Athena heard a group of coyotes sounding off somewhere below. She spent a moment or two determining their location, all the while watching Sam's behavior. If Sam had decided to pay them a visit, she would have accompanied him, as chasing coyotes is one of her favorite pastimes. Sam was also tracking the pack, and decided the coyotes deserved a respite from his normal response.

Athena gave Sam a look that begged him to step into action. That particular glance from Athena usually worked. This time, however, Sam showed no interest except to monitor the coyote pack's travels to ensure they weren't tailing the hiking group that happened to be several hundred yards in front of them. As tentative coyotes passed us below on the game trail, Athena decided to give them a holler. She belted out a very wolf-like howl, and immediately the coyotes disbursed. The hikers looked everywhere but up, and hastened their movement down the trail, presumably counting the steps to their waiting vehicle. Athena and Sam listened for a coyote response, but no recall came from below, and we didn't see or hear from the coyotes again that day.

Not far away, in a suburban part of the greater Phoenix area, daughter Lisa was beating down the pavement with her favorite running partner Marli. This was a nearly everyday occurrence for the pair, and both Marli and Lisa enjoyed the respite from the day's typical requirements for each participant. Lisa's morning would be spent performing various tasks associated with the graphics design portion of her company, and Marli had the task of protecting the domain they both called home. It was a day like any other, except for what happened next.

Marli Learns to Surf

Lisa and Marcel had a treat for Marli. No guarding the house for her today. Marli had amassed quite a few medals for various extremely difficult dog-related activities revolving around agility training tasks. She was ready for anything.

It was time for something completely different. After a short training period, Marli was released into the emerald water with nothing but a surfboard and a ton of agility. As you can see by her expression, she had absolutely no fear—only a ton of reluctant confidence.

It goes without saying that Marli, had a nice evening's sleep in store for her at home.

Sam, Athena, Milo and Marli make a most exceptional pack, each having their own unique characteristics. This is wonderful, particularly when you realize that each one of them is a rescue animal whose previous owners either abused or neglected them. Imagine what goes through each of their minds when they awake every morning to this new and enjoyable life none of them could possibly conceive before.

The Pack

Sam, Athena, Milo and Marli all get along better than well. Each has a unique way to look at events that pass between them, making each hike or adventure a wonderful first-time event. Here are a few examples.

The Pack

One fine day, Marli decided to come and visit Sam and Athena. Milo was already in attendance, as Angie let Milo stay with us while she visited her parents in a distant land called the East Coast.

Marli, being the new kid in town, was treated as a newcomer in a Federal Penitentiary would be, as everyone's plaything. She went along with it for a while, then turned the tables on the group by establishing her type of dominance.

She quickly had a discussion with Athena, who was all ears, though not ears like the pair Marli sports, but that's another story. Once the girls were in agreement, the tables turned very quickly.

Sam and Milo had a pair of dominant females to deal with, and as anyone who is married to a dominant female quickly realizes, it is no longer the fifties. The year two-thousand has come and gone, and the current set of rules cater to mutual equality on more levels than anyone in the fifties imagined could ever exist.

That said, Athena and Marli quickly took charge of the morning's excursion. First, they set the boys straight by teaming up and handing them a serving of their own medicine. After that, things settled down, and everyone enjoyed a morning of chasing and cavorting around in beautiful Sedona landscapes.

Girls Against Boys

Now that things are balanced between males and females, it is time for a bit of fun. From a human perspective, it was a free-for-all, gender independent. Wild creatures. And so, once again, domesticated animals found their wild side and let it out for a bit.

And So, Once Again

Now that you have met the pack, let's enjoy some of their experiences together.

Sam Teaching Milo How To Swim

CHAPTER 2
Sam and Milo

S am, on one of his more playful days, decided to allow Milo to see his favorite swimming hole. Milo, fully understanding Sam's propensity for miscreant behavior, approached cautiously. With significant precautions in place, Milo took step after step, not realizing that Sam was positioning Milo exactly where he wanted him.

As Milo came into position, Sam swiftly moved to Milo's side, and gave him a love tap in the general direction of the currently unmanned swimming spot. Needless to say, Sam got his way, and Milo went tumbling into the pool of water immediately below.

"Next time, I'll be the one in the saddle!" Milo thought to himself, as Sam watched triumphantly from above. Sam, oblivious to Milo's sentiment, was already planning his next assault.

Yes, Milo would be more cautious of Sam's miscreant behavior the next time, but most certainly, Sam would be even more careful to plan his next bit of trickery. The two of them spent a moment studying each other, with the small overhang between them being the only deterrent to a bit of wrestling and discussion of the recently passed event. Milo thought about knocking Sam around a bit but remembered the last time he tried to do so. That attempt had not been successful.

It doesn't take much to capture either Sam's or Milo's interest. Over the hill nearby, the sound of a singing coyote family could be heard. As if nothing had just happened to assault Milo's sensibilities, he and Sam took off as one toward the disturbance, presumably to show the awaiting coyote group who was boss in this small bit of earth in a small forested area in the land of Sedona.

As the coyotes signaled each other, Sam and Milo got into position. Only when both were set did Sam signal the attack. Within seconds, both had consumed the mile or so between the coyotes and these two scurrying aggressors. The coyotes did the right thing, and separated in a disorganized pattern of retreat, presumably to reassemble later, after which they would share some heated discussions about the incident.

Sam and Milo returned to the company of their two caregivers, Mike and Angie, who missed out on the chase. Both canines were in a state of satisfied exhaustion, and proceeded to request whatever treats were on hand. Now, a short trip back to the swimming hole was in order.

Sam and Milo Cooling Off

"Good chase." Sam thought to himself, as he pounced in Milo's general direction.

Milo watched, a bit bemused by Sam's behavior. Milo had come to know what was in store when Sam was around, and appreciated the attention, even though it often meant getting hammered around a bit. During this exercise, Milo was giving Sam a lesson in temperament and anger management, and Sam was gradually becoming more tolerable both as a pet and human companion due to Milo's influence.

The relationship was making life enjoyable for the human caregivers Mike and Angie as well. Exercise is the gift these two knuckleheads brought to their caregivers, and the most valuable gift anyone can receive. With health comes the ability to live long and prosper, as well as be a good example for the remainder of humankind.

After the brief swim, the small group headed back to the trailhead, a few short miles away. Once there, Sam and Milo retired to the back of the Jeep, and recounted their adventures while drying off on once clean and dry portions of the Jeeps interior. Soon thereafter, both Sam and Milo decided to take a respite from the day's activities. The couch seemed to be the appropriate recipient of their attention, so thereupon they both came to rest.

Sam and Milo Taking a Break

How Milo and Sam Met

One day, a visit to the dog park began a friendship which would forever change Sam's life, and that of Milo. This is the story of Sam and Milo's first meeting.

Sam was very well known at the small school yard which doubled as a local dog retreat, one of very few places in Sedona where pups of all sizes could meet and discuss their respective lifestyles and gripe about their human caregivers. Sam was the unofficial protector of small dogs, and the little ones would rush to his side at the top of a small knoll, where they all could review the other dogs playing and wrestling about with no fear of attack.

On this particular day, a very large but timid Milo entered the yard, and he was immediately attacked by a group of very aggressive dogs, who meant no harm, but nonetheless seemed a formidable source of discomfort to Milo.

Sam, reviewing the activity from afar, decided he didn't like the introduction Milo was receiving, and he launched from his position of power, intersecting the path of the group of aggressors. Once Sam came into view of the approaching horde, the group immediately found their brakes and came to an abrupt stop. For a brief instant, only Sam was on the move. He stopped at Milo and gave him a welcoming nod, and both Sam and Milo retreated to the grassy knoll, where the smaller pups welcomed Milo with open paws.

The group of wild dogs resumed their play, as Sam and Milo watched, comforted by the presence of a dozen or so smaller happy faces. Milo became a regular visitor at the dog park, accompanied by his rather attractive caregiver, Angie.

In time, Angie and Milo became eager attendees of Sam's daily hikes in the greater Sedona area, and a pattern of happy days became the norm for both Sam and Milo.

Angie With Milo

Sam's First Haircut

It came to pass that Sam was experiencing some discomfort due to the length and thickness of his angel-hair soft fur. His coat seemed to be made of extremely fine and bountiful fur, rather like a cat than a dog.

This we assumed was a mutation of the thick hair found on a Golden and the soft fur located on the underside of a coyote. Mike decided to take him to a local pet store in Sedona, knowing that the groomer who inhabited the facility had a penchant for taming the wild beast in any pet which required and did not necessarily enjoy grooming.

True to form, Sam whined and fidgeted through the entire process, but seemed to be more active and eager to play once several pounds of hair was removed. Being properly fed and watered, Sam asked to take a brief trip to the nearest wooded desert area, where he turned on the speed without fear of prematurely becoming overheated.

After the hair removal procedure, Sam seemed to acquire a significant amount of additional energy, due to the removal of excess hair, and made a nuisance of himself with the denizens of the bit of earth beneath his freshly groomed paws. He was able to run significantly faster than the day before, finding numerous little creatures that needed a bit of exercise and training in predator avoidance.

A quick measurement of Sam's running speed with a GPS device showed he was moving up to 45 MPH, and then beyond for brief periods. Even the evasive jackrabbit was no match for Sam's speed, but Sam seemed more interested in chasing rather than catching, so all wildlife in the area was spared the inevitable fate between predator and fleeing prey.

Looking at Sam from the chase victim's standpoint was something affected creatures most definitely would remember forever. His eyes seemed to glow as he pumped up the forward velocity. With his winter coat long gone, Sam became the epitome of speed and control, and was quite a sight as he ate up mile after mile at an unheard-of pace.

On this fine day in Sedona, Sam became a bit faster, and he knew his new-found ability would come in handy when it was necessary to engage the wily coyote pack which shared Sam's favorite playground.

In the meantime, Sam would be satisfied with chasing Milo around the forest, finely honing his predator pursuit skills. Milo, on the other hand, would have to tolerate yet another form of Sam's miscreant behavior. Fortunately, Milo was very adaptive and extremely tolerant of Sam.

Milo had his own skills, and could easily jump over the speedy Sam, leaving Sam grabbing a bunch of air rather than Milo's backside. The unique arrangement between this pair began to form a lifelong bond that the two of them would share for a very long time. Sparring became a routine activity, and both Sam and Milo improved their cognitive skills and intuitive capability as they played aggressor and victim. These skills have allowed them to survive and control numerous visitations from Coyotes, Bobcats, and the infamous Javelina packs abounding within the Sedona wilderness.

Sam Wreaking Havoc

Angie Finds Milo

Sam and Milo would have never found themselves together if the following events failed to occur. Fortunately for Sam and Milo, there was Angie.

Angie, being a thoughtful but resourceful individual, decided to think seriously about bringing Milo into her world. She continued to ponder how mellow and cute he was, in that basket of wiggle-worms, and with the continued insistence of workmates, she finally caved in and brought him home. As it turns out, the love between Angie and Milo blossomed like a spring flower, and has outlasted relationships, cars and jobs, and continues to be the standard by which lasting relationships can be measured.

Milo came into the picture as a very young puppy. Angie first saw him in front of a Home Depot store wearing a purple vest inscribed with the words "Adopt Me". It was love at first sight. Little did she realize he would grow, and continue to grow, until he reached a stature matched only by the possible exception of a very few rather large canine breeds.

As Milo grew in stature and personality, Angie realized she had made a most exceptional decision in bringing him into her pack. He has often proven his mettle in protecting her from the infamous UPS driver and more importantly, the shoe-fly.

Milo Posing

Milo has travelled many times with Angie as she searches for the best place in the world to settle down and plant roots, each time without a complaint or issue. He continues to find the best in each place they land, and Milo provides the consistent type of companionship humans require of their best canine friends.

Like Sam and Athena, Milo is consistent and predictable in his behavior, which means he is the ideal companion for an active and forward moving human. All three of them seem to know how humans feel, and they also seem to know exactly how to make the pains of life and living go away when we need them to most. Humans as a species need something that can ease the stress of our everyday lives that doesn't take pill form or require surgery, and canine companions are one of the best medicines currently available.

Milo Finds His Place in Angie's World

Angie, Milo's caregiver, has a most unique job, which allows her unlimited access to some of the most beautiful and pristine hiking areas in the world. Milo, whose exposure to unlimited fun and entertainment was somewhat curtailed prior to meeting Angie, quickly found out how lucky a once homeless pup can be.

That fact, coupled with the wonderful food and seemingly unlimited treats available, made Milo strongly believe he had crossed over and become a heavenly denizen of the next chapter of his journey. Life had changed for Milo, for the first time.

Once Milo and Angie found Sam and his pack, things changed again. Sam became Milo's best buddy, and hiking with a friend became the norm for both Sam and Milo. To this day, the two are inseparable, and can be found hiking together as one entity in the beautiful forested areas near Sedona.

Milo shares a wonderful gift with Angie; the undeniable present called unconditional love. This wonderous treat has carried Angie through some extremely tough times as she grows and assumes ever increasingly complex roles in her chosen profession. As the two of them move forward on the path of life, Milo steps up during difficult times and gives Angie the necessary boost in confidence and inner strength needed to move on to the next life event. Whether it be a demographic change or upward move in the workplace, Milo is always there for her.

Spirit Wind

Living in Sedona and the neighboring area has a profound influence on a being's inner strength. The Force is strong here. Many humans experience a spiritual awakening while visiting, and some of them stay and become part of the spirit wind that passes over this land. It was so with the original natives who inhabited the area, and it remains so with many more recent denizens, both human and otherwise.

Laura

Angie's friend Laura is one with the spirit wind and has the capability of sharing the strength she acquires with others in need. Along with Milo, Laura helps Angie work through occasional issues that happen at inconvenient times and overwhelm. Laura can see the imbalance and has a way of smoothing out the rough edges, making various annoying issues dematerialize. It is an amazing gift which Laura is willing to share with those in need.

Laura With Angie

Visitors have been flocking to Sedona to find spiritually connected healers who will, in turn for a handful of money, cleanse them and make them better people. Unfortunately, this has created an opportunity for certain not spiritually inclined humans to take advantage of them and undermines the work of the few spiritual beings living here who have a gift to share.

The true healers are not in a little shop with junk hanging about for sale that will cure all ills. They are not sitting in a vortex conveniently located just off the trail or road. They live among the people and keep to themselves until called upon. They will find you if your needs are genuine and without ulterior motives.

Angie, Milo and Sam

Long before Athena came into the picture Sam and Milo ruled the forest. Accompanied by Mike, Sam's caregiver and Angie, Milo's caregiver, the two boys experienced a multitude of interesting excursions into seldom seen Sedona scenery.

Angie, Milo and Sam

On this fine sunny day in Sedona, Sam directs his pack to a small group of six coyotes travelling on a trail below. The coyotes are oblivious to the trio of watchers as they track a couple with a small white dog in tow. Angie immediately sees them.

Milo gives the predators below a warning. The pack immediately disperses, as they know Sam and Milo very well, and decide the small white morsel in front of them is not worth getting a visit from Sam and Milo. A few days before, Sam and Milo introduced themselves to this group, and for the coyotes, the meeting did not go as expected.

Sam and Milo, and the select group of canines they bring into their pack on occasion, hold a special place in this forested area of Sedona. Many other hikers with dogs in tow know the pair well and are relieved when they see the Sam and Milo pair patrolling the forest.

Many of the predators in the area also know the pair, and their behavior with other canines and their caregivers has been adapted to make pup hikes a much more enjoyable experience for visitors, residents and their special canine friends. That is the gift Sam and Milo, and the other pack members, bring to the area called Sedona.

Javelina are a most interesting species. They are unpredictable in behavior and mannerisms and are extremely territorial. They like to bite and gore potential adversaries, and as a result, should be avoided, both for your protection and theirs.

A few days ago, Sam and Milo were on patrol, and were amusing themselves with a chipmunk who had taken up residence inside a hollow tree. They heard a quiet movement behind them and were confronted by a huge javelina. The huge pig-like creature wanted to start a fight.

Sam and Milo have never started a confrontation, but are more than willing to stop one, and somehow conveyed that fact to the awaiting aggressor. And so, without any effort on their part, they resolved the conflict by giving the Javelina a meaningful stare. The javelina decided he would take his fight elsewhere.

Sam, Milo and Javelina

As the Javelina backed away and then trotted off, a peaceful feeling came over the pair. Another conflict avoided without incident. Both Sam and Milo were happy the situation was resolved without any aggression from both parties. Now it was time to return to the chipmunk, who was chirping away, still hidden securely in the impenetrable tree trunk he and his family called home.

Yes, Sam and Milo started the relationship that brought the pack together. Many other canines have joined, and this book will describe pictorially and with a few words some of these unique treks. Sedona is the backdrop for most of these tales, and no place on earth has the special power this small piece of the Arizona wilderness possesses.

Sam and Athena's First Hike

CHAPTER 3
Sam and Athena

Some days are nice and normal; this one was to be most exceptionally different.

Sam and Athena Meet

Sam was not happy. We were heading in the direction of the shelter where he was originally housed when we adopted him. Little did he realize, we were not taking him back, but getting him a new sister.

Athena had been here in the shelter for about a week. It was her first time in such a place, and she did not approve. Her previous owners had determined she was too much for their lifestyles, and had a friend dump her at the shelter under the premise that she had been found wandering about the neighborhood.

Athena had been intentionally bred for a Sedona family from a Mexican Gray Wolf and a Siberian Husky. Mom was the dog, and her dad was a tame wolf. The family quickly learned that you don't go to work and school and leave an intelligent young wolf hybrid alone with your valuables.

The first evening everyone returned home, they didn't recognize the place. Nothing was as they left it. Things from the living room were in the bedroom, and vice versa. Cabinets had been opened, Kleenex boxes emptied, closed doors opened, including the front door, and Athena was long gone. This went on for about a week.

And that is how Athena became a denizen of the Sedona Pet Shelter.

As we pulled up to the shelter, Sam looked at us with a stern expression indicating that he wasn't going back in this place. We got out, made our presence known, and an attendant brought Athena outside and located her in the outside visitor area.

Sam sat up and took notice. Linda asked Sam if he might want to go visit this youngster and Sam's expression and demeanor changed immediately. We took him over to the enclosure and watched from outside.

Athena watched Sam's every move from the safety of the fenced area but displayed no concern. Sam, in turn, watched Athena walking around, and decided he wanted to join her. We accommodated Sam and let him enter the enclosure.

What happened next was a Sedona miracle. Two unique hybrids got acquainted and became friends, putting aside the Coyote way and the Wolf way. It must be true that opposites attract, because a strong bond and visceral connection came out of this short meeting in an extremely brief amount of time.

The first hike was another miracle. Athena put away her flight instinct and ran with Sam. Wherever he went, so went she. It was amazing to watch, and even more exciting to participate in their enjoyment of the venue.

After Sam and Athena's First Hike

Afterwards, it was to the human bed they went for a little nap prior to asking for a nice dinner. Sam was considering hot dogs and grated cheddar cheese, and Athena was ready to accept pretty much anything except dry dog food. This was the Harris household. It was needless to say that they both got their wish.

The first hike with friends turned out to be equally remarkable. With so many different personalities in the mix, I feared there would be one or more issues to resolve. Fortunately, Sam turned out to be the mediator, and all went well.

Sam, Athena and Bon's Pups

Shortly after Athena and Sam became friends, we got a visit from Angie and Milo. For Milo and Athena, it was love at first sight. To this day, they can't be separated.

Sam, Athena and Milo at Play

Milo has a way about him that girlie dogs can't resist. This gift helps him navigate through the pack carrying a significant amount of respect and admiration. Most of the females in the pack enjoy his company and like to hang with him during rest periods. Athena is no exception. She will do anything to capture his attention.

Milo With Athena

But then, Athena likes to pester anything with four legs and a tail, so any pups who hike with us becomes fair game, particularly if they can run fast and true.

Athena Trying to get Sam

It is not unusual for Athena to tackle any unsuspecting hiking pup just to see if he is watching for her. Sam is typically the recipient of this form of attention, but Milo and any other pup she is familiar with can become the prey at any moment.

Another day in paradise brings yet another adventure for the pack. Milo is here, Sam is here, Athena is here and another pup visiting from far away joins the fray.

Marli, Lisa and Marcel's pup has a rock and roll activity level, which fits in nicely with Sam and Athena. Milo, somewhat more casual, is fortunate enough to have long legs and unlimited stamina, so he can make the best of these three knuckleheads as they chase about, looking for someone (Milo) to pester.

Milo's Welcoming Committee

Today, Milo is the designated victim. As he exits the vehicle, the welcoming committee is prepared to give him a bit of exercise. Milo drops out of the Jeep, cautiously surveying the situation. He picks an exit route through a small clearing in the brush, and dashes forward at top speed. Marcel, Marli's caregiver can barely keep Milo in sight as he sails past and over to the main trail.

Milo is now the hike leader. He keeps a comfortable distance ahead, monitoring the hectic activity behind him as Athena, Sam and Marli swap roles as aggressor and victim. For the time being, Milo is safely in front, a position he has come to love.

As the hike progressed, each pup; Sam, Athena and Marli took the role of aggressor. Milo watched carefully from a comfortable distance. He knew it was only a bit of time before someone noticed him trekking well ahead of the group on today's designated hiking trail and made the decision to initiate contact.

Milo Becomes the Prey

Athena was first. She closed the distance between Milo and the group in a few fast bounds, but Milo was already alert and picking up speed. The others joined in, and the hike progressed with most of the pups well out of sight.

After the Chase

After the chase, a few of the participants found themselves atop an ancient Native American prayer spot as the sun began to rise above the neighboring hills. It was time to rest and refuel. The morning's effort had taken its toll on aggressor and prey. Now it was time to relax and plan the next adventure. One of the pups decided that maybe a visit to the local creek crossing would be an appropriate venue, and the remaining canines and hybrids readily agreed. It was about a three-mile hike to the water, a distance the group crossed in a few short minutes.

Sam's Girls Frolicking

Sam Pestering Milo

The water was cool and refreshing, prompting the group to renew their antics. A small toy was found, and the girls teased Sam with the small object for a while. Sam became significantly friskier than before, and went after Milo, who had found an isolated pool of still water in which to relax. His rest was interrupted by Sam, who decided to use the pool and rocky area surrounding it as a playground. It wasn't long before everyone joined the two, and another chase through the forest was initiated.

Activities like this were new to Athena. She had a lot of adapting and learning to accomplish in a very short time. This was a critical time in Athena's development, and she knew it. Being an extremely intelligent creature, she was up for the challenge.

Athena quickly acclimated to the Harris household and the numerous guests who enjoyed hiking with them. Every day brought a new adventure, and Athena quickly gave up her unique methods of obtaining attention, such as chewing up Jeep seat belts, hiding food, digging up the backyard in order to find things she once buried, and chewing on wood furniture.

This change in behavior sealed her a permanent place in the pack and made her a valuable member at the same time. Sam came to love her, and since the feeling was mutual on Athena's end, life for both hybrids turned into a delightful thing for all of us to share.

Athena Initiates Play

It wasn't long before Athena started taking the initiative in the pack's activities. She rapidly became a prime instigator in various activities, creating a game called "Let's get Athena."

The object of this game was simple. The pack member who could catch Athena would find out how quick she could turn the tables and become the aggressor. This fact did not diminish the desire of each pack member to give chase, even though each one of the pursuers knew the outcome would result in Athena reversing the roles.

Sam was the notable exception. When Sam caught up with anyone he was chasing, the victim would learn something new about combat tactics. Athena was not excluded from this rule, and often came back from a hike extremely dusty or dirty, as a result of what Sam did to her once she was caught.

Sam Gets Athena

Athena did find that most of the pups who hiked with us tended to be more pliable than Sam, and she enjoyed testing each one as they became introduced to the pack. Jess was no exception. He would join the hike white as a sheet, and after the hike he would resemble Sam in color. This was typically Athena's doing, and was one liberty Athena took from Sam, the typical instigator of such behavior.

Today's hike gave Athena significant opportunity to give Jess a good working over. Jess, who matched Athena's exuberance and love for the forest, was a perfect target for Athena's behavioral anomalies. Little did he realize the full extent of Athena's trickery.

As Jess trekked about looking for things of the forest, Athena prepared for the attack. Sam, who normally calls the shots on most of the walks, decided to hang back and watch, a move which turned out to be the best possible option.

Athena Tackling Jess

Jess turned around just in time to catch Athena on the attack, and carefully avoided getting hauled to the dirt. This time, he was diligent in avoiding Athena's forceful advances, but he knew the likelihood was great she would find another opportunity.

Sam Protecting Jess

Meanwhile, Sam was watching the entire scene with interest. He had plans of his own involving the new pup on the scene. As Athena charged Jess for the second time, Sam walked between them and Athena put on the brakes.

Sam led Jess over to a nearby place of shade and they both found comfort in Athena's newfound humility. As they rested and talked about the day, Athena found something else to occupy her, and off into the woods she leapt.

Jax Free at Last

It came pass that a young pup from far away came to visit Sedona. He stayed with his grandpa, a retired Marine with a heart of gold. Kevin was the perfect walking companion, carefully keeping Jax on lead as they traversed through the forest.

It also came to pass that Athena and Sam were in the immediate demographic region, and the three of them began to frolic in the Autumn mist, sans the dragon and cave. Kevin, seeing the nature of the play, decided to give Jax a fair chance, disconnecting the lead.

Upon doing so, he saw the full measure of the capabilities of Sam, Athena and Jax, and was quite amazed. He realized, however, that if Sam and Athena decided to run off for a couple hours that Jax would probably accompany them. This, coupled with his love for Jax's owner, compelled him to restore the link that connected him to Jax, and the fun was over for the day. I decided to add this bit of pictorial proof in order to allow Jax to relive this brief moment of freedom, and perhaps bribe grandpa to allow this event to be duplicated at some later point in time.

Jax Free at Last

Sam's First Trip to the Sea

CHAPTER 4
Sam and Pack

Sam is definitely the leader of this group of misfits and has quite a few stories. All, of course, are shared adventures with one or more of his pack members, and whoever we could coax to join. Most of these sensory treats occur in the Sedona area, however some are the result of travels to interesting and beautiful locations that we found elsewhere on the planet.

On an isolated beach near the Mexican border in a small town called Imperial Beach, an aquatic-oriented feathered creature decided to go for a swim. Sam became interested in inviting the petite creature for lunch and decided to give ocean swimming a try. Little did he realize that the salt water he needed to traverse had some unusual characteristics. One of them was wave action.

Sam watched the bird, who was focusing on his own version of a noon meal and didn't see Sam's inquisitive gestures on the shore. Both creatures were focused on their idea of lunch as the waves came in and broke at Sam's feet. The first few of them backed Sam up repeatedly, and then Sam decided to take the leap.

Sam took a mouthful of the water, and immediately gave it back up. He looked up at me as if to say, "You could have given me a heads up about the salt!"

I laughed a bit, and Sam ignored me, returning to the task at hand. He jumped over a couple of waves and began to swim at a rapid rate. The bird, finally noticing Sam's interest in him, finally took flight, leaving Sam and the waves behind.

Sam Swimming the Ocean Blue

Sam found himself relatively far out as the next wave approached. He didn't seem fearful, and successfully rode the wave back to shore. Once his feet hit sand again, he turned around and repeated the process. After a dozen or more rides, he was sufficiently tired, and we returned to the awaiting vehicular conveyance.

Back to the Jeep

Unique adventures are not a Sam exclusive. Marli, for example, has quite a few stories of her own to share. The surfing incident is but one of her many acquired skills.

One extremely warm day the pack went to a local swimming hole located below Cathedral Rock, the most photographed place in the land of Sedona. An amazing thing happened. Marli took flight in a manner unlike anyone else in the pack had ever experienced.

Marli Sailing

Athena was transfixed, Sam was completely amazed. It was a most triumphant feat. Marli easily leaped over twelve feet before landing in the cool clear water. To this day, she still holds the pack record for distance jumping.

Milo is not without skills. He can run like a deer, and we recently found out he can leap like one as well.

The day stated out normally, with an early morning hike in a forested area south of the land of Sedona. The area was teeming with life, and there were numerous exciting chase scenes to be had by all canine participants. One such chase started with a chipmunk dropping out of a tree amongst the pack.

Sam was the first to notice. He initiated a chase which carried the pack to another nearby tree, but this tree already had prior occupants. When the current occupants of the tree noticed the converging pack, each chipmunk took off in a different direction. Every one of the fleeing creatures had at least one canine on its tail.

Milo's fleeing victim got sneaky. It turned on Milo and ran up his chest, launching itself in the direction of a nearby tree. Milo followed suit and jumped nearly six feet to grab the little rascal, but barely missed. He then was faced with attempting to execute a safe landing. As Milo prepared his descent strategy, the chipmunk settled in at the treetop and watched, satisfied that he or she had successfully evaded capture.

Milo Flying

As the day progressed, Milo realized he had earned a new merit badge for his feat of amazing flight. Accolades came from Sam, Athena and Marli. Milo was extremely happy with the newfound respect he earned, and he felt more at home with this unique pack of adventurers.

It wasn't long before Athena and Marli began to toss each other around and display their true colors. A chase ensued, with Marli playing the victim and Athena in the role of adversary.

Marli was extremely fast and kept Athena on her toes. As Marli ran rapidly down the path, she began to take corners at an extremely high speed. She was confident that when she slowed and looked over her shoulder Athena would be far behind or would cease her pursuit, but she was entirely incorrect.

Athena was right on her tail, chasing Marli into the tight corners with exceptional skill. Mike and Marli's caregiver Marcel watched in amazement as the two creatures approached them at blazing speed, passing by within a few moments of each other.

Athena Chases Down Marli

Athena did finally catch Marli. It was quite a sight to see. Both girls do have skills.

Marli vs Athena

Marli made an attempt to capture Athena, but Athena had a different idea. Before a very excited Marli could wrap her up in a ball, Athena shot out from under her with a burst of energy, and soon disappeared behind a nearby tree.

Sam came over to Athena, and they conversed, then Sam and Athena decided to hand Marli some giveback. Brother and sister converged on the unsuspecting Marli.

Marli Surprised

Marli took off like a lightning strike, but Sam was on to her immediately, followed by Athena. The two of them had caught the high-spirited Marli, and for the time being, the chase was over.

And It Happens Again

And so, the inevitable happens. Athena, who never likes to call it quits the first time, decided to engage Marli again. This time, she let Marli take a huge lead on the hike, and then tracked her, as wolves do. Marli, oblivious to Athena's trickery, was moving through the tall grassy area without a care in the world. Sam, not far behind, knew exactly where Athena was located at every instant in time.

As the grass thinned out and Athena became visible, Sam made eye contact with her. Athena continued stalking Marli for another hundred yards or so, and then decided to make her move.

Athena rounded the last bush in the clearing and closed on Marli. Athena's victim didn't see her until it was too late. Athena looked like a wolf with an empty belly as she came into view, and Marli immediately jumped in the opposite direction, but it was too late. Athena had caught her off guard.

And So It Happens Again

Fortunately for Marli, all of Athena's actions were just in fun, and she quickly toned down her aggressive stature and the girls began to play once again.

Visiting Milo was the next one to feel the wrath of Athena. She waited until he was engaged in a contest with a rabbit and snuck up behind him while he was focused.

Athena After Milo

After the rabbit was long gone, Milo had to deal with the rapidly closing Athena, a situation that often found its way into Milo's daytime activities while visiting the land of Sedona.

Milo turned up the speed and dashed across the grassy field, trying to put some distance between the pair, but to no avail. Athena already had a running start and was rapidly closing the gap.

Athena Lined up on Milo

Athena Gets Hers

Athena had sufficiently pestered all the hiking pack on this cloudy day in Sedona whose sky suggested a near-term rain event and was settling in for the hike back to the vehicle. Marli decided the day's events were far from over and showed Athena the full measure of her decision.

As Athena started to relax into her wolf-like lope, occasionally scanning the area for something of interest, Marli got into position. Both Sam and Milo saw what was happening and kept their composure, so that Marli's plan could reach fulfillment. It was a perfect plan about to be executed in a most exceptional manner.

It is safe to say that Athena didn't have any clue and was completely unprepared to be the victim. Marli took aim and got Athena on the ground immediately, and without a significant amount of effort. Athena, who is never tricked twice, added this little bit of training to her roster, in case someone decided to give it a second try.

The rest of the hike back to the vehicular conveyance was relatively uneventful. All three pack members behaved, as if their breakfast of oven roasted turkey followed by a substantial treat made of something that once adorned some form of livestock was dependent on their behavior.

Now it is Athena's Turn

After every hike of significant length there is a nice meal, followed by an extensive rest period. All pack members participate in this event.

Sam and Athena at Rest

Sam and Athena finally settle down for a much-needed rest after an interesting day.

Athena After the Geese

CHAPTER 5
Amazing Places

Some amazing places have been visited by our hybrid family. Here are a few.

Today was to be an extremely special day for Athena. She determined that she had the capability of swimming, and not only could, but actually excelled in the skill.

Athena Hunts the Geese

In a land far away called Colorado, a clear clean basin of water came into view during an early morning hike. The narrow trail circumnavigated a grassy field which contained the attractive body of water, and soon we were walking among the cattails and other foliage while watching a large group of geese swimming nearby.

Suddenly, we heard a splashing sound to our left. As we looked over the tall dense growth of vegetation that surrounded the pond, we noticed something swimming alongside us. It was Athena, in her maiden voyage as an aquatic mammal.

She swam at an amazing rate, all the time her head held high, as if looking for something. Then we saw the receding group of geese ahead and to her left and knew her objective.

By the time we realized her intentions, she had swum to the center of the body of water and was nearly undetectable in the mass of feathered creatures swimming slightly slower than her. Finally, they broke into flight, and Athena, realizing her prey was long gone, swam back to the shore a few feet in front of us.

The Source

While continuing the hike, we decided to try and find where all this water was originating. It seemed the thing to do, since we had no other objectives planned for the morning, and we knew the pups would love some additional time on the trail.

The Source of the Water

A long hike later, we came across a stream that was fed by a huge waterfall. It was so high above us it was difficult to take in while walking, so we took a seat and looked above. The water was becoming vaporous as it plummeted to the rich earth below, and both canines and humans were transfixed by the beauty of this spectacle.

Soon after, Sam decided it was lunch time, and found a nice place to sit and consume mass quantities of the sustenance we provided him. Immediately thereafter, he considered and then accomplished the fine art of relaxation.

Lunch Time

After the brief respite, the hike continued with a return to the awaiting vehicular conveyance. This was one of many days in paradise that Sam, Athena and Milo would enjoy on this trip.

An Earlier Trip

During a trip to Kanab whose objective was to spend time with Angie, we had an amazing thing happen. It turns out that you have to participate in a lottery in order to obtain access to a hiking area called North Coyote Buttes AKA The Wave.

Angie and I decided to try this one alone due to Linda's condition and the temperature. We felt it might be too much for the pups, and that was a good decision, as it was over one hundred degrees at the site once we reached our destination.

The lottery picks on the first day did not include our number. On the second day, I told Angie to plan on going. She was a bit skeptical, and once the first six out of ten participants were selected, was convinced we would not be participating.

I looked at her sad face and told her we would be picked, and I was right. To this day, she wonders how I knew.

The drive to the trailhead was pretty rough and rattled the Jeep around quite a bit. We saw people in lesser vehicles parking along the road, deciding to hike rather than destroy their personal motive devices.

Once we reached the half way point, out of the sandy creek bed grew the most amazing features, and immediately we were grateful for the opportunity to view this magnificent feat of nature.

Entrance to The Wave

As we climbed out of the sandy wash, the full magic of this serene place embraced us. A newer form of serenity than I have ever experienced fell over me, and I could see Angie go through the same process.

Among the Spirit Winds

Then the sun moved into the canyon, and we could feel the full measure of ancient presence here and we listened quietly to the spirit wind singing the songs long ago forgotten by the early Americans who once traveled through this mystical place.

This was an adventure I will not soon forget, and the insight I received from the spirit winds here will remain with me for many years to come.

Finally, as we exited the area, we passed through one remaining canyon before dropping back into the sandy wash leading back to the trailhead. The spirit wind sang one final song to us, reminding us of the magnificence of nature, and asking us to do what we can to preserve it for generations to follow.

Spirit Lookout

The last formations we could see as we walked back to the wash were reminiscent of ancient warriors keeping watch over this sacred place. They were well positioned in a power spot, and the pair of monoliths kept a diligent gaze over the wondrous formations we were leaving behind for others to find and appreciate. Hopefully visitors in this time and those who follow will respect, admire and protect this place and others like it for all time.

Weaverville and the Firestorms

2015 was not a good time to be in northern California. The forest was on fire, and nothing that could burn was safe from the wind and the firestorms it fed. We were in a small community visiting Angie, who was working in the area, and were mystified by both the fire and the resilience of the local inhabitants during this very tense period of time.

Every evening, the inhabitants would assess the firestorm's progress and make the decision to stay or leave their homes. Then, in the early morning, the same group of survivors would review the progress once again, before deciding whether to go to work or pack up and leave.

Fear of Impending Doom

Finally, the huge helicopters arrived, and utilized the nearby water supply to push the fire off the mountain. In a few days, the smoke subsided to non-dangerous levels, and life returned to normal.

Aftermath

Once fires were under control, life began again. Sam and Milo joined Angie and me, as we traversed the forested area which remained unharmed, and began to relax. Angie and Milo knew the area very well and had numerous trails and water-laden places in mind to show us.

The first was a remote site where a lookout point for the USFS was located. Upon first glance, the road looked impassable due to the high percentage of grade in the steep climb. It was definitely a road only a capable 4-wheel drive vehicle should consider navigating. As it was, walking up this steep gravel-laden path took significant effort, and once atop the hill, it was equally challenging to descend.

Man and beast could see miles from this access point, and while there we selected some nice places as hiking destinations, all of which had a measure of water. This was a necessity, as our pack was in need of some water-based activity.

Lookout Point

We quickly made way to the nearest site with aquatic options. Angie and Milo tested the water temperature and deemed it acceptable for both human and beast.

Water Sports

This was a perfect beginning to a most exceptional morning, as Sam pondered entering the slowly flowing stream. He did not consider the decision very long before taking action.

Once Sam made his way into the cool aquatic paradise, things took a different pace. The placid water took a much more turbulent state, as Sam practiced his predator skills, and Milo, not really having a vote in the matter, became the prey.

Milo's Turn

Then Milo, urged on by Angie, decided to turn the tables. It was quite the thing to see as Sam, dropping the role of aggressor, allowed Milo to chase him through the churning mass of water. Milo was feeling his oats as he gave Sam a good run, at least until Sam decided to reverse roles again.

This, like so many others, was an extremely adventurous day. The pack would long remember this as a great day. All of the pack members have been exposed to less than ideal situations in the before life, and each member is grateful for the gifts provided by their respective caregiver. Now for a quick rest before the return trip.

As caregivers to unique creatures like Sam and Milo, we derive the benefit of regular exercise and the discipline necessary to maintain the health and well being of our pack. In this manner, we create an extraordinary relationship with our pack, and both human and canine entities benefit.

Now it is time to seek shelter and consider resting a bit. Then, a meal fit for a king will be served, and discussion of the day would ensue. After that ritual, Sam and Milo would seek out and find an appropriate position in the domicile to rest, where each of them could keep an eye on the household they have come to know and love.

A Brief Rest Before the Trip Home

Naptime

The Bond between Sam and Milo would bring together other humans and canines, and set the standard for other packs of humans and canines to use as an example for their own relationships based on love and adaptability. Good days like this are the building blocks for long term successful relationships between differing species.

Closer to Home

Sedona has its own unique set of features, unlike those that can be found anywhere else. Sam came to us with familiarity of many places he had visited during his time alone in the forest and was more than willing to share them with us.

Ancient Travelers

In a place very near Sam's current domicile, there exists evidence of the existence of prior denizens to this unique area called Sedona. On the walls of certain canyons can be seen beautiful and strange images created by the travelers as they visited and lived here for a brief period. The stories they tell are of contact with forms of wildlife, some of which no longer exist on this planet. They also tell tales of great hunts and tragic losses to their tribe, and some pay tribute to great hunters and fellow members who excel at their crafts. Some even depict geologic and weather events that captured the attention of the tribe members.

Kokopelli

Kokopelli, the fertility deity is often portrayed in these petroglyphs. Here is one example. He shares space with horned lizards, coyotes, deer and the infamous sabre toothed tiger, in nearby images on the same side of the canyon face. Within a few hundred feet of rocky hiking a visitor to this area can find hundreds of images in various condition based on exposure to sun and the other destructive elements.

This area's indigenous creatures can sometimes be dangerous to humans, so tread lightly and watch where you place your feet. It is not unlikely to see one or more vipers of the rattlesnake variety slowly meandering about. One trip to the area, while taking pictures like these, a huge western diamondback rattlesnake slithered over both of my feet, presumably in search of a delectable rodent to consume.

Hungry No More

This rattlesnake was one of the lucky ones. He had just begun to consume a recently caught morsel, and by his girth, he had a couple more in his stomach. Snakes mating are considered to be a blessing to many ancient populaces. It is often that the ancients who once populated the area we call Sedona will depict this act in the artwork they placed with care on these canyon walls.

Snakes Intertwined

Interesting but Harmless

One of the most unique denizens within the ecosystem called Sedona is the Horned Lizard. This reclusive creature was also revered by the ancients and is seldom seen in the present day due to habitat destruction by bipeds.

The Horned Lizard has earned its place among the Sabre Toothed Tiger and the mating snakes on the walls of the canyon we are navigating today as the pups enjoy a swim in the fresh clear water.

Horned Lizard

I am blessed to have seen a couple of these creatures in their natural habitat and am hoping that they will continue to survive and perhaps prosper in those areas where humans fear to tread.

As populations of humans invade these sacred places, they can cause irreparable damage to the native indigenous species. Fortunately, the USFS has guidelines for travel through and within the wilderness areas, so places like this will remain safe from harm for our descendants to enjoy.

While reviewing the petroglyphs and discussing them with some of our party, I was surprised to hear one of them say they had never seen a Horned Lizard, stating that they had lived in the area for two decades. As he pondered the image, I searched through the pictures in my phone, which number in the thousands, and found a couple of pictures taken nearly ten years apart, both of this unique creature, and showed him both. To this day, he is convinced that I fabricated the images, and remains adamant in his belief that they do not exist.

Horned Lizard 1

And, about ten years later, we found this little guy about fifty yards from the original location. These are the only two I have seen in the area of Sedona.

Horned Lizard 2

It is interesting to note that the coloration of each Horned Lizard matches the soil and surroundings to the extent that I believe it is adaptation to provide camouflage as a form of protection. Both soil types can be found a short distance from each other.

Hiline

One of Sam's favorite hangouts is a trail that starts in the Village of Oak Creek and winds past Cathedral rock, dropping down to several trail options below. The trail has several remarkable viewpoints which look down upon some of the best features in the region of Sedona.

Sam loves to lead this remarkable journey and has welcomed numerous humans and canines to join in and enjoy the scenic magnificence of the area. Angie and Milo were the first to join in this expedition.

Angie and Milo on Hiline

Hiline has spectacular views of Bell Rock, Cathedral Rock and the entire west side of the VOC. It connects with Transept and Baldwin Trails, and provides a most exceptional hiking and biking experience, as long as you don't mind exposure to steep cliffs. A mistake on this trail and your only option is a helicopter ride.

This section of the Sedona area trail system is unique, and very attractive to bikers and hikers. Sam is happy to invite other pack members and their caregivers to this beautiful location, and often does so. One of the most enjoyable areas is a left-hand turn which takes the trail directly in front of Cathedral Rock.

There is a social trail that leads to the upper plateau of Cathedral, but it is not clearly marked, and not suggested for the tennis shoe clad hikers who normally walk this trail. Instead, take the left-hand turn which leads to Baldwin trail and hike down the double black diamond bike path. It is a tough hike and a very challenging descent if your mode of transportation of the day possesses two wheels.

Cathedral Rock from Hiline

On one nice spring day, Sam found a hiking buddy called Jess. Having a shared lineage, both pups became friends immediately. Time to show Jess Hiline.

Playtime

After a bit of running around with Jess, Sam decided it was time to show off his favorite playground. A short drive followed by a moderate hike brought Jess's family to the most photographed feature in the Sedona forested area.

Picture Time

Everyone except for Sam and Jess brought out their cameras. Cathedral Rock posed silently in the foreground, as it had done for numerous centuries before, and quite probably would for a significant number more.

A Hangover in Sedona

There is a video rolling around in the social media arena which depicts a unique experience in the Sedona area not connected with man's desire to abuse controlled substances sold legally in liquor stores. The highlights of this video contain extreme biking skills on an extremely well-exposed trail called Hangover. Originally built by the greater Sedona area biking community and formally recognized and supported by the local Forest Service engineers and staff, this trail has become internationally recognized as one of the best biking trails on the Continent.

It is also an extremely enjoyable hiking experience, and one that Sam particularly likes to share with fellow quadrupeds and their biped caregivers. There is a definite spiritual presence here, if you have the ability to observe and walk the narrow trail without fear of falling. When the wind blows here, travelers feel an incredible lightness of being, which gives them the feeling of weightlessness, something that makes the narrow trail feel ever smaller in stature.

Everyone who hikes with Sam on this trail, including Athena, comes back with a sense of accomplishment unlike anything they have experienced, and the experience becomes one of their favorites. The pictures do not give the happening justice. You must experience it personally to get the full benefit.

What's in There

I tried to get Angie to crawl into this mini-cavern, but she was four-square against the idea.

This, and several other unique features make Hangover a nice experience, including the well-weathered areas sculped by the wind and rain. The name comes from those sections where the rocky cliffs above literally hang over the trail. In some places, this happens in a most inopportune manner, and the hangover closes the gap bipeds need to traverse the section.

Bikers on the trail, if over five foot in height, might have a bit of a problem traversing these sections, as the gap between the ceiling and floor decreases to less than five feet. Having ridden these sections on an extra large bike, with my height being over six feet, I can identify with this issue.

The drop from this place is several hundred feet. It is not a good idea to approach the trail edge, as it often erodes suddenly taking the occasional hiker or biker with it.

Angie With a Hangover

Despite the exposure, Hangover continues to be one of the most enjoyed trails in the greater Sedona area. It is constantly maintained by the Forest Service and volunteers from the Verde Valley Cyclists Coalition and Friends of the Forest, two local volunteer groups.

On this particular voyage into the Sedona scenery, the spirit wind was stronger than usual. Voices came from the trees, and they were clearly celebrating the wonderous day we had in store for us. There was reason to travel cautiously, however, because the same welcoming wind that stole away the strong heat waves was the same wind that shaped these unique features.

Each turn on the winding north face brought another huge gust of wind, and the heaviest of us (me) felt uncomfortably light in the strength of these forceful windy torrents.

We finally had to find a relatively flat place and sit out the strongest portion of the advancing gusts. As we stared into the source of the atmospheric anomaly, we heard the voices again. As the ancient elders asked us to tread gently on their homeland, we looked down and saw the swaying trees as they marked the gusty torrents advancing on our location. The treetops swayed in huge waves, reminding us of the ocean, and those who watched were transfixed by the uniformity of the wind waves, which were amazingly similar to the wave action in the ocean.

Spirit Windy

As the wind subsided, we were pleased to realize that the spirit wind was here for a purpose. The message we took away from this experience was to stop and enjoy the moment, as there will never be another like this, and missing it would not be good.

Athena and Jess on Hangover

Just Checking In

CHAPTER 6
Things of Beauty

S am has been witness to many new and exciting things. Here are but a few of them.

On this fine sunny day while accompanying his caregiver on a bicycle trek into the forested area surrounding the land of Sedona, a visitor from the past came to check in on her terrestrial charges. She sailed silently on wings of silk, landing on a small portion of the bicycle piloted by Mike. Sam watched silently and felt the presence.

Mike thought about this a bit, and then realized that this day was the anniversary of his mom's death, and the time was approximately the time of her crossing over so many years ago. She waited a while, and then took off in a northerly direction, never to be seen again.

Sam watched the event as it unfolded and realized that something he had always considered to be true actually was a truth. He listened to the spirits in his new home often, and when he slept in the room nearest the front door, he could feel the presence of those long gone from here, and often he laid in the exact spot where one had crossed over. The presence there brought him comfort and a measure of serenity.

He thought they came back in other forms but was skeptical until this day's event came to pass. Once he saw Mike's visual response to this visitation, his suspicions were confirmed. From this day forward, Sam would look at such events and realize the magic of such visitations, even though he might not know the reason. It was comforting to him that once he left this place, he might be able to return and visit.

Mike was having one of those days. Things were not moving along well, and he decided to take a respite from the things of man, so he and Sam took a long trek into a familiar yet desolate porting of the Sedona landscape nearby.

While taking a brief rest, both Mike and Sam pondered the day's events and were deep in thought when it happened. Just like before, a small visitor circled their area briefly, and then landed on Mike's gloved hand.

Mike felt the warmth immediately, and Sam was aware of the sensation via his contact with Mike's senses. Sam knew this was a good thing for both of them.

Answer From Within

As the small creature climbed about on Mike's hand, the answer came to him. It was a life changing decision, and to this day, Mike is grateful for the help this beautiful creature his higher power sent provided.

Sam, who was a believer, was excited and happy his caregiver had been given the answer and rejoiced as both Sam and Mike returned to their domicile to share the good news with Linda. As events unfolded as a result of this decision, it was evident that the visitor had a good grasp of events that would come to pass and was willing to share the essential information with Mike.

With each visitation, Sam became more aware of how things in this world worked, and he became capable of helping in ways only he could. When he sensed stress or indecision in Mike or Linda, he centered on the problem and if he could, influenced decisions that would make all of their lives move more smoothly. He had finally become a true member of the pack.

One bright and shiny day, while walking through some taller than normal grass, Mike discovered a small chrysalis that had fallen from a tree above. Sam, who decided not to eat this tender morsel, was more than willing to let Mike take it home. Both were eager to see what would transpire as this small mummified creature began its new life.

The next day Mike and Sam returned to the same area and were horrified to see that some idiot hunter had left a campfire unattended, and a small grass fire was the result.

It was easy to extinguish with some dirt and a shovel, but the damage had been done. A hundred-year-old tree was the primary victim. Both Mike and Sam were angered at this stupidity and did what they could to try and determine who had caused this offensive event to pass. Nothing remaining yielded any clue however.

Back at home, a miracle was in process. Mike and Sam returned to see a beautiful creature on the wall above the plant where Mike had anchored the chrysalis.

Life After Death

Both Sam and Mike forgot immediately about the sad events in the forest, and instead rejoiced about the new life they had helped create. The fire would have consumed this beautiful creature whether or not it had remained in the long-gone tree. Sam was beginning to understand the way of the Great Spirit.

As he drew a smoky breath there in the smoldering forest, Sam decided he was extremely privileged to witness the miracle of creation, and to this day, he will not eat anything that resembles a caterpillar or chrysalis.

Bending the Light

Long ago, Sam determined he had the capability to tweak a universal constant. He was looking in vain for some intangible item, and decided he could use some help, so he drew upon a gift he had not used to date. He concentrated on the source of light available and pulled some down, and finally found that which he sought.

Sam Bends the Light

Sam and Athena Stir up the Universe

It is not uncommon to witness this occurrence when Sam's busy chasing his Athena, as Angie and Milo found out on a recent hiking opportunity. The sun was sinking low on the horizon, and darkness was imminent. As the two hybrids, Sam and Athena, began to dance about causing havoc, the light suddenly bubbled up, allowing this brief respite from sanity to occur and be readily visible. Then, as suddenly as it appeared, the light went away, and it was time to find the vehicular conveyance and depart the scene.

Athena Tweaks the Light

The next day, Sam was surprised and pleased to find out that Athena was beginning to understand the gift of the light, and how to use it. I watched, and silently hoped these two knuckleheads wouldn't upset the time-space continuum enough to cause a worldwide disaster.

Meanwhile, the rest of the world went along as if nothing had happened, and all was well. Sam and Athena continued to play with the light until a rabbit came out of the brush to see what was happening. Immediately the focus of both hybrids focused on the rabbit's activities, and a chase ensued.

After the day's activities, everyone returned to the Jeep, and from then on Sam reviewed Athena's behavior in a different light. He gave Athena his prized place on the couch, and now allows her to initiate play without knocking her around like before. Athena is currently the alpha in the pack, and Sam makes certain all others who interact with the pack understand this important fact.

Both Sam and Athena were exhausted when they arrived home, and each had a bit to drink followed by a nap. Both snored like I've never heard before. It was a good day.

More Things of Beauty

Sometimes the Great Spirit has a bit of fun when it creates an environment for us to see and appreciate. Such a place can be found in every location where humans and their non-human companions dwell. Within these sites can be found living things unique in appearance, and beauty.

Wind Sculpture

Sam and Athena both have a most exceptional gift that allows them to appreciate beauty in many things, and they are willing to share their findings. Every trip into the wilderness brings something beautiful to experience.

Sam has a penchant for finding and sharing flowers and other living things. He will locate something of beauty and then seek his caregiver out. Once he locates his person, he walks slowly towards the object, watching to ensure he is being followed. He displays his finding with a smile and wag of his tail.

Athena is different. She will often grab the thing of interest and bring it to her companions. Sometimes this has a significant effect on the condition of the finding. She is a work in progress in this behavioral tendency.

One day Athena found an antler shed. She quickly hid it in a cactus bush where no one could see it. Sam knew where it was, but since he had decided Athena was to be the pack's alpha, he allowed her to keep it to herself. This lasted for about a week, then she had to investigate. Upon finding the shed had been moved by something, she reacquired it and decided to share it with us. Unfortunately, she found out how good they taste and ate two horns from it before sharing. Sam, of course, just smiled and reminded himself that it was hers to share, not his.

That very same day, Sam shared some things of beauty himself. "Humans like this stuff.", Sam thought to himself, as he shared several items unique to this demographic region.

A Pretty White Thing

Another One

Sam really knows his stuff. These delicate things of beauty are as hardy as beautiful.

Michael and Linda Harris

Just Checking In at the Shelter

CHAPTER 7
Sedona Sky

Sam has always enjoyed a great sunrise. Today's was no exception.

Something wonderful was about to happen today. The sky lit up like something on fire. Sam saw the sky this way one other time. It was the day he checked himself into the Sedona Animal Shelter to get his bad case of giardia cared for. He had just finished an early morning breakfast at Col. Sander's Chicken and was sitting on the front porch awaiting the first person to arrive.

But that was then and this is now. What was in store? He had to move on with the day's activities and just wait and see.

The morning hike went well and without incident. Sam was getting impatient, but never showed this aspect of his feelings. Something was most certainly going to happen. Once loaded back into the Jeep, he could feel it, and then it happened.

Mike drove back home, but didn't offload Sam. Instead he picked up Linda, and the three of them progressed northward. Sam was showing his interest now, and Linda said something to him, but he didn't get the meaning of the conversation.

Then, Sam realized where they were going. He hadn't been there in years. Was he going to change caregivers again? This would most definitely not be acceptable in any manner whatsoever as far as Sam was concerned. This was definitely going to be a memorable day in everyone's eyes.

Everyone got out of the car, but thankfully Sam was allowed to remain in back. Maybe he wasn't going to have to live here after all. He could only hope at this point.

Then, Mike came from the building. He opened a gated area in front and asked Sam to join him there. Immediately afterward, something amazing happened. Linda came from the building with a beautiful creature in tow.

She was like nothing Sam had ever seen in his entire life. Athena was her calling, and she was part canine but also part something else—something very wild. She reminded Sam of the internal conflict he experienced every day, being part canine and part Canidae. He felt her anxiety and fear.

Athena Arrives on the Scene

Athena walked over to the edge of the enclosure and reclined. Sam cautiously approached, in order to give her time to scent him. He marked several plants and then waited patiently a few yards away, all the time making eye contact with her.

Athena rose, and walked over to the spot Sam marked, smelling while keeping him in her sights. She marked where he did, and then walked over to Sam. They did the scratch and sniff thing, and suddenly they were friends. Within a few minutes, they were romping around in the enclosure together.

Needless to say, Athena rode home with us, and has been at Sam's side ever since. They engage in play constantly, and hunt as a single unit, each of them taking cues from the other as they herd prey. The nice thing is once they capture, they release the prey unharmed. After all, there is oven baked chicken or turkey awaiting them.

Sam Plus Athena

On another day a bit more recently, Sam was gazing at a beautiful sky as he awaited his caregiver's preparation for the morning's excursion into the great Sedona wilderness. Something's going to happen. Sam thought to himself as they began to trek about in the sparsely foliated area near a local trailhead.

Something's Going to Happen

True to form, Sam was correct in his vison. After the hike, on the way to his current domicile, Sam looked out the window and saw something amazing that he had never seen before. It was a most exceptional happening, confirming his senses were right.

That What Goes Up Must Descend

A huge flying thing was on the ground near the road back home. It looked as though it had ceased to live, collapsed there on the ground. Sam witnessed many of these things while hiking and could hear voices coming from below huge sphere. He always wondered what they were, and even this close to one, his senses told them that they were not of the living.

No voices came from this one. It was getting smaller as it sighed softly, and sounded like the life force was being drawn from it. Several humans ran about, seemingly helping it cross over. Once they were done, the thing was collapsed to a much smaller form, and quietly carried away.

Sam finally decided that, like the Jeep, this thing was a method of conveyance for caregivers. He was somewhat relieved to determine this, since before this time he had always considered them to be huge predators, somewhat like the owls or other raptors, and that they should be monitored closely. This conclusion gave Sam a newfound sense of security, and he felt one step further up the food chain as a result.

Time for Something New

Another beautiful sky greeted Sam as the sun took its place in the eastern sky. Shining from below the cloud layer upon a slowly growing storm cloud in the west, the sun created a sense of change in Sam's mind. Expectations began to develop in Sam's sensory organs, and a waking dream set upon him.

Time For Something New

Sam manifested a newer method of conveyance, one which had more space dedicated to non-human passengers. He saw new adventures in store, with many fellow canine participants able to be present as a result of this change.

Sam's New Wheels

Today they turned a different direction from the way home. A few minutes later, Sam was riding home in a new vehicular conveyance. It was as Sam had envisioned.

Sam Takes Off

CHAPTER 8
Linda's Stories

Sam and Athena share a special bond with Linda, one well worth a mention.

These stories, written by Linda, have a certain flair that only Linda can properly communicate. Like the previous chapters, the stories start with Sam.

Sam's First Walk With Momma Linda

Sam was a new gift to us. On the card attached to his enclosure at the humane society was one important phrase. It read "escape artist".

I kept that in mind when we brought him home. I reminded myself that it wasn't about building a taller fence, it was about building a home he didn't want to leave.

I knew I had to consider everything I planned for Sam with this in mind.

Mike had returned to San Diego for business purposes so it was up to me to take Sam for his first hike in the forest. We have a hiking location where there are hardly ever any other hikers.

I parked the Jeep, let Sam out and quickly attached a leash. I might have lassoed a moving train and had less resistance. He dragged me over cactus and rocks, down through washes, up and down until I couldn't move another step. Off in the distance I heard a familiar voice. Our friend Rick and his collie Brooke, who was also known to take off without permission, popped over the hill. I was so glad to see him, I was rescued!

Rick took the leash for about 6 seconds and let him loose. OMG! Sam took off and I was sure I would never see him again.

We saw what the tail end of a cottontail rabbit followed by the fast-moving hindquarters of both dogs. The last thing we saw was a cloud of dust.

After a few minutes we realized we were transfixed and holding our breath. We looked at each other……I finally uttered "Mike is going to kill me".

It was a good 15 minutes before we saw what we thought was Brooke. Here she came, walking slowly up over the hill…we waited. I called to Sam again and again and then here he finally appeared. He stayed with me the rest of the walk and even jumped into the jeep when prompted.

This good boy got ice water and a treat in the Jeep and a well-deserved nap when we got home. When Mike called that night I kept my description of the day short and sweet. Just that Sam had been a good boy.

He always has been and still is over a decade later. My beautiful, nutty, soft buddy.

Sam Helps Mommy

"The stick Sam, bring Mommy the stick."

It was a beautiful Sedona morning without a cloud in the sky. A warm 74-degree spring day. Sam and I were out for a hike in a part of the forest accessible only by Jeep. This was the beginning of a wonderful excursion.

The hike started out as usual. I asked Sam which trail he wanted to take, and we were off. We progressed across the meadow and down into a wash, and then up the hill. Half the way up, I seemed to lose my balance. Down I went, sliding on the still damp grasses and rocks; lots of rocks. All of my gear went flying, my walking sticks one way and my water bottle and gun went another and my phone was under me.

I tried to get up and fell down again. What's going on here? I tried again with the same outcome. Again, and again I tried to crawl to my walking sticks for assistance, but the terrain kept me back. I cried to Sam to bring me a stick. He did immediately and with no avail. I was stuck and the cuts and bruising I received on impact started talking to me. I didn't like what they were saying. Sam was licking my face; I felt better.

I picked up my phone to call Mike. Our daughter Lisa was up from Phoenix for a bike ride and I should be home by now. I looked at the phone's screen. No signal.

If I waited where I was, eventually Mike and Lisa would come looking for me. For right now the sun and Sam coaxed me into taking a nap. An hour or so passed, Sam didn't leave my sight. It was time to try again.

Still no signal with the phone. With the help of one stick and Sam I was able to stand up.

I was very wobbly, but I was up. I was, with Sam's help, able to get back to the Jeep. I tried the phone again and got a signal but no answer.

I drove home and met Mike and Lisa in the garage. They got me into the house, cleaned me up and put me to bed with Sam by my side. He never left me.

Sam Protects Linda

Bringing Home Baby

The phones began ringing early Thursday morning. Mike and Sam were out for a hike, so I tried to take the message from a half-hysterical caller. It seems there was a wolf hybrid puppy that needed to be rescued.

Mike and I are part of the Wolf Conservancy project and support our local shelter. These two facts were about to collide in one beautiful Siberian Husky/Mexican Wolf girl hybrid named Athena. Athena, in mythological times meant "Goddess of War" another aspect of the little bundle that rung true.

The calls kept coming in. It seems everybody who knew us wanted us to come to the aid of "Athena".

That said, we returned calls and collected information. She was just one year old, a Husky/Wolf bred for sale, bought by a Sedona family, abused, exhibited destructive behavior and about to be turned in to the local shelter.

This is where I came in. I called the Sedona Humane Society and told them what I knew.

They remembered us from Sam and the articles I wrote for their column in the local paper. What I asked them to do was to let me adopt her sight unseen. There were things that needed to happen before we could have her, like bringing her to date on her shots, spay her and give her a wellness check. There was a disturbing condition which couldn't be found during the standard checkup however. Her knee was later found to be damaged, probably from the abuse.

Three weeks later, the checkup and a pile of paperwork finally complete, we got the call. We could bring Sam to the shelter for the final test, a meet and greet between Sam and Athena to see if they were compatible. Sam loves all of God's creatures, so it was up to the new girl, and us of course; we had never seen her.

Out she came with her head down and looking so sad that tears came to my eyes. Her coat was dull and she was grossly underweight. I knew all these things could change with a good diet, regular exercise and socializing. This would allow her to realize she was safe from any more pain and most of all, open her mind for lots and lots of love.

Sam gave his wag of approval. He could see her pain. She let him kiss her face and then herd her towards Mike's jeep for the ride home. I took Sam in my car, so he could once again be reminded that he was still top dog.

Athena Finds Her Place

Upon arrival home we introduced her to one room at a time, then the "doggy door". She entered our bedroom and immediately jumped up on our bed and curled up and put her head down. She was home and she knew it. So did Sam; that was his spot.

Athena learned the house rules comfortably. Well almost. It's about the doggy door. We had been letting her out and she was used to doing her thing on her hikes, but the first time I saw her use the doggy door I stopped in my tracks! There she was with her head and both front feet through the door and her back end still inside standing in a puddle of pee. I wanted to laugh so hard my sides were aching. I gently suggested that next time she go clear outside. That would work better for both of us.

Then, suddenly, I was laid up in the hospital for several months with a bone disease, so I missed some of Athena's escapades. Mike came to visit daily told me the latest.

Athena didn't like me not being there and Mike occasionally working at Absolute Bikes or going for a bike ride and leaving her at home. She did not like being alone and getting constant attention.

One of the days Mike was at work Athena got bored. This is not a good thing. The leg of the all-wood Armoire became her victim. She started chewing at it until she ate into a strip of metal used to join two sections. Looking around, she noticed other wooden tidbits, including the little wooden knobs. By the time Mike got home, the damage was done and thee of the knobs were missing.

One morning when Mike decided to go on a bike ride early instead of taking the dogs out for their daily 4-mile hike, he came home to find his hiking shorts and socks shredded to bits with Athena standing in stiff defiance.

During the next few years she grew up and mellowed. As Mike says, "she has finally settled in".

Still limping and holding her back leg up while standing, the issue with the hind leg needed to be addressed. We took her to our veterinarian and the tests began. X-rays showed a blurry mass at the knee extending up. We gave permission for minor surgery to obtain a positive diagnosis. As it was, with just the X-rays, it looked like ether valley fever or cancer, which would mean losing the leg.

The surgery went well and all 8 of the biopsies were on their way to Phoenix.

Finally, we got the call with the news. Benign and not a sign of any disease. Thank God. She would continue to limp when the leg was cold, but you can't catch her when she takes off across the forest. The doctor said that it could have come from an injury, signifying a sign of physical abuse. That hurts my heart. To remedy the situation, the doctor prescribed a treatment plan including glucosamine and chondroitin.

Several months passed. Mike finally got both of his overused knees replaced so we asked our friend Kevin to take Athena and Sam out for their morning hike. After a longer than usual time had passed, Kevin called to tell us that he lost Athena.

Mike and I got in my Jeep and headed for the trailhead. Kevin needed to get to a meeting, so I left Sam and Mike to try to get to Athena. It had only been about a week since his surgery, but Mike insisted he walk with my walking sticks and look for her.

When I returned from dropping Kevin off, I kept calling her name, a desperate plea which carried through the canyons for miles. I also wrote a description and our cell number and gave it to every hiker I could find, and then posted a note at the trailhead. We waited, I cried, Sam whined.

Three long hours later here she came, tired head hanging down. She had taken after a heard of Javelina, (looks like a wild pig). She must have gone miles, and finally exhausted, made her way back to the Jeep. We imagine that she stopped several times to rest. It was a warm Arizona morning.

After we got home, Mike got online and ordered a tracking collar. She loves it like a special necklace. Now she insists on having it put on before she goes for her hike. We can track her for over 10 miles. Haven't needed to use it since, but after a scare like that, it was the thing to do. A little like insurance for our little adventurer.

Athena is 3 now, twice her original weight, sporting a bright and shiny coat, healthy and affectionate.

Mike took her out the other day and something we have waited to hear finally happened. A pack of coyotes in the distance were howling, informing those who cared, that they were there.

Athena Howling at Coyotes

There was Athena in all her glory reaching her head towards the heavens howling a wolf howl. The coyotes stopped.

The queen was here. She let out another long howl.

Sam smiled, saying to himself: "That's my sister."

If someone were to leave a special Christmas present under my tree, it would have to be a little golden puppy with huge feet named Sam. He came to us this way, bringing gifts of immeasurable value, saving lives, saving souls, gifting layers of hopes and dreams, reassuring those who have lost in love in the past, all the time wearing a glowing presence around his head like an old tapestry. We all should remember that we have these same abilities. Sometimes it takes a special visitor to remind us to watch and learn, and then pass these gifts on to others.

Lightning Source UK Ltd.
Milton Keynes UK
UKRC020922290119
336229UK00004B/109